BRAVE FLYER

How to End Your Fear of Flying

By Michael Salem

Written in the United States of America

The Author is the sole owner of the intellectual property of this book.

This book is not intended to provide or replace any medical or psychological advice. Readers are encouraged to seek the counsel of professionals with regard to the impact on their mind, psychological, or medical wellbeing of such matters discussed in this book, or the impact of travelling by air to their mental or physical conditions. The Author specifically disclaims any liability, loss, or risk of any kind incurred as consequence, directly or indirectly, of the use and application of any of the contents of this book.

Testimonials

"Avoided flying for years- Now I am perfectly comfortable being on-board a plane." Trae Hyden

"For the first time ever, my heart does not race and I am not nervous during take-off" Janet Sanders

"I can finally eat, enjoy a movie, even sleep while on a plane. Thank you Michael!" Haylee Alan

"First time I read a book on Fear of Flying where the Author seems to know exactly how I feel" Diana Hanson

"Well Done, Well Written!" Nick Adeeb

"Fears are nothing more

        than states of mind."

Napoleon Hill (1883-1970) American speaker and motivational writer.

TABLE OF CONTENTS

ABOUT THIS BOOK

This book takes a refreshingly different look at what is known to many people as Fear of Flying, a supposedly distinct and independent phobia related to being on a flying object, most commonly a plane. The book reveals that such a phobia does not even exist, which explains why most people who try to rid themselves of this phobia through conventional methods such as reading books or attending therapy programs, or through alternative methods such as hypnosis, fail. Simply put, they are trying to treat a non-existent phobia.

So you ask yourself, 'Why am I scared about being on a plane if there is no such phobia?' Well, in my opinion, most people who avoid flying are not sure of the reasons why they are afraid to be on a plane. They think they suffer from a phobia known as "Fear of Flying", because that's what they were told or have read. If, and only if, they know exactly what is scaring them about being on a plane, the chances of overcoming that fear would significantly increase. Simply put, they would understand the root cause of their fear and be able to treat it.

You see, what is known as a "Fear of Flying" phobia is nothing more than an end result, or a symptom, of one or more underlying fears that present themselves as a single phobia. Depending on the individual, these fears can be related to heights, loss of control, or enclosed spaces.

In addition to the underlying fears, there is another powerful and equally important cause of fear of flying, and that is what

I refer to as 'external elements'. These are the very normal and routine events that take place before or during the flight that cause the anxious flyer to become more alert, and subsequently increase his anxiety levels. Examples of such events are the closure of the cabin doors, the fasten seatbelt light coming on, or even the 'ding' sound that the pilot uses to communicate different messages with the flight crew.

This book will concentrate on these 'other' fears and external elements, which are the sources that need to be recognized and dealt with independently in order to eliminate any issues or concerns you may have when boarding a plane.

From my research, I have learned that most fearful flyers are not overly concerned with the possibility of an airline accident. This is exactly why statistics that tell you how driving a car is more dangerous than being on a plane, or how well planes are engineered, will do little to calm your fears. The risk of flying is not the issue here. This emphasizes the fact that there is no such thing as a "Fear of Flying" phobia, if nothing else; the term is inaccurate, because nervous flyers are not scared from flying itself (although they might not recognize this fact).

The goal of this book is very simple, and that is to help you lose your fears and anxieties about flying by showing you how to identify, understand, and treat the root causes.

The book has two main areas of concentration. The first deals with the most common sources of your fears and how to eliminate each one of them. You will probably identify with one or more of these fear sources. The second area is a step by step method that starts with planning your trip and ends with you being on board a plane. Think of this section as a hand-holding guide on what you should do.

INTRODUCTION

WHAT IS FEAR OF FLYING?

There are estimates that over 30 million people in the United States alone have some sort of fear associated with flying on a commercial jet. The level of anxiety varies significantly, ranging from minor uneasiness all the way to a paralyzing fear that prevents people from even getting on a plane.

As I mentioned in the introduction of this book, there is no such thing as a Fear of Flying phobia. The so-called phobia is actually just a symptom of other fears. For example, a frightened flyer might be suffering from claustrophobia (fear of enclosed places), acrophobia (fear of heights), or agoraphobia (fear of open spaces), or any combination of these phobias. When one adds in the unfamiliar sounds of the engine and any air bumps during the flight, a complex situation arises that is hard for anyone to properly identify as a single condition, so they commonly refer to it as a Fear of Flying. Simply calling this complex emotional feeling "Fear of Flying Phobia" is a naïve and misleading to the victim.

When I ask a fearful flyer about the reasons he or she avoids traveling by air, nine out of ten times I do not get a clear answer. They simply state that they have a phobia about flying. I believe that they honestly don't know why they are afraid of flying, and as long as they cannot pinpoint the source of the problem (and therefore simply call it a flying phobia), they will not be able to treat it. It is like calling up your doctor and telling him that you are sick, without even mentioning what part of your body is hurting. This is why many fearful flyers are not able to rid themselves of their anxiety; they simply do not know what to get rid of in the first place.

So unless you open up this mysterious mental box that you have labeled a Fear of Flying phobia, and take a good look at what is inside, you won't know where to begin or what to treat. This book will help you open it, understand the contents and deal with those fears.

ABOUT THE AUTHOR- AND YOU!

For so many years, I could have easily been the spokesman for the 'fear of flying' club, if such a thing existed. I was a genius at making up excuses just to avoid traveling by air, excuses such as medical issues; fabricated work schedules and meetings; visiting family, and even funerals of already dead family members. (I cannot even remember how many times my grandfather 'died' in order that I need not get on a plane.)

When excuses were not an option or had been overused, I would try to convince friends and family to fly to my city instead of me flying to theirs. However, this trick did not always work, or it would be very inappropriate approach. For example, it was obviously a very odd request to ask a friend to come over to see me to celebrate the birth of their son.

This fear was taking a huge toll on my personal life. You see, the problem was that although I loved to see new cities, mountains, beaches, or visit friends and family, it was out of reach for me as many of these destinations were simply too far for me to drive to. I had friends I had not seen in years; I missed weddings, anniversaries, and reunions, all because I would not get on a plane. And how bad did I feel when I saw those vacation commercials and getaway discounts that my pocket could afford, but my emotions could not?

The impact did not end at the personal level - it was also affecting my work and business life. It was difficult and embarrassing when I had to come up with a new excuse every time my management requested that I travel for a meeting or for training. This not only made me look unprofessional, but had a negative impact on my career. In many cases I ended up recommending someone else on my team to travel instead of myself - talk about a career limiting move.

For many of you that fear flying, the above could have been written about you as well. The stories might vary a little, but the core of the problem and its impact are the same.

It is very important that you read this book with the right attitude, where you are telling yourself, 'I can control my emotions, they can't control me'. I know that a person who is scared of flying can easily make up excuses and pour negativity on anything or anyone who tries to help him or her overcome their fear. Believe me, I was once that person. So when you read through the book, don't allow the negative part of your brain to tell you something like, 'Oh, this does not apply to me,' 'This is just talk,' 'He is just trying to make me feel better,' 'Easier said than done,' 'This is not 100% true,', and so on. Be positive.

CHAPTER ONE: FEAR FUEL - THE 3 EVILS

This chapter discusses factors that can negatively contribute to your existing fear of flying. I consider these influences to be a type of fuel, strengthening your belief that there is something inherently frightening about being on a plane. Properly dealing with these elements could very well be the difference between winning and losing the battle against your fear.

The good news is that the 'Three Evils', as I like to refer to them, can be controlled by you. They are generated either through your thought processes or from an external influence that you can choose to ignore, unlike other factors that you have little or no control over, such as air bumps for example, which is an actual event where you have no choice but to experience when they occur. This can be compared, in a way, to weight loss programs. Many experts ask overweight people (who are trying to lose weight) to eliminate certain components that, if left unaddressed, will simply make their weight loss efforts that much harder, and possibly fruitless. For example, dietitians will advise their patients not to watch food commercials, avoid walking in the snack aisle at the supermarket, avoid discussing delicious but fattening dishes with friends, and even avoid thinking about unhealthy food cravings.

The same applies here - to ensure a successful recovery journey, you will need to first eliminate some bad habits or avoid certain situations. If it proves impossible to avoid them, then you will have to train yourself to ignore them or give them as little time and attention as possible. But prevention is easier and more effective.

Once you eliminate these factors, or significantly reduce them, you can start working on putting an end to your flying fears, as now your fear has lost its fuel supply.. Once a fear is dead, then it's dead for good.

MEDIA

Media has been and will continue to be a great source of information and one of the greatest wonders of our civilization, but when it comes to fearful flyers it can be one of the biggest sources of anxiety.

In general, mainstream media strives to follow dramatic events - they really care less for the regular and mundane happenings that actually make up over 90% of our daily lives. For example, your evening news would almost certainly mention the two or three major accidents that took place during rush hour that evening, but would never report that 10,000 cars safely made it home from work - that wouldn't attract anybody's attention. Simply put, dramatic and rare stories sell better.

The same applies to airline reporting, but on a different scale. Unlike car accident coverage, the media cannot report only on major airline accidents - years might pass before having something to report on. So in many cases they have to magnify minor incidents, which, by the way, are also scarce, in order to fill the air time. Suppose one day a plane skids off the runway with exactly zero casualties. This incident will become breaking news with big red letters and scary impact sound effects. And yes, you guessed it - never a word would be mentioned that there were thousands of successful takeoffs and landings that very day, and thousands the day before, and the day before that, and so on, and so on, for months and months back.

When this sort of news coverage is heard by someone who is frightened of flying, you, for example, your fear will increase exponentially. The image of being inside that plane while it skids off the runway, with objects being thrown all over the cabin and people screaming, takes over your brain waves and imagination and translates into more fear. But when you give the rational part of your brain an opportunity to think about it, you will realize that this news is actually an opportunity for you to reduce your fear of flying. Does that sound strange? This is how it works:

The fact that this fatality-free skidding story got so much attention is very simple - it is such an unusual event for any flight to encounter any issues, that every news outlet wants a piece of it. It's almost as rare as a UFO sighting (actually UFO sightings are more common than airline accidents). If planes skid off the runway every day or even every month, this kind of news may earn a spot on the back cover of newspapers, if nothing much else is going on that day.

There is a very interesting media fascination with commercial air transportation. The media just loves covering stories that have any connection to an airline or airport - and believe me, it has nothing to do with the high frequency of airline crashes because that is simply not the case. For example, both the plane that skids off the runway without any casualties, and the cargo airline that catches fire after landing will get heavy international media coverage that can last for weeks. On the other hand, a horrific car accident that tragically ends the lives of two families will only get local media coverage that evening and will never be covered again.

So be smart and rational next time you hear about an airline incident on the news. Keep reminding yourself that the coverage is only there because it is such a rare event. If you want my honest advice, detox your brain and stop watching the news altogether.

ACTIVE IMAGINATION

The term might have many meanings depending on the situation being discussed, and in some cases it is a positive activity. But in this book, an active imagination refers to a phenomenon where fear is created or exponentially magnified by self-generated negative images and catastrophic scenarios. It is worth noting that active imagination can be triggered by an actual physical event or by a previous occurrence of active imagination.

For example, for a fearless passenger, a seatbelt light means just that - time to put the seatbelt on. At worst, this person might take it one step further and worry about the coffee spilling because this sign indicates that there is a potential for the typical air bumps to take place. You see, there is no active imagination at work here.

Now, let's take the same example above and apply it to a fearful flyer (you). The seatbelt light being turned on, which is an actual physical event, is a trigger for the active imagination. Once the seatbelt light is switched on by the pilot, your imagination takes over and you start seeing images in your brain, sometimes very vivid, of how the plane will shake you relentlessly and you will start hearing some people screaming. This is an active imagination triggered by an actual event.

As mentioned in the beginning of this section, active imagination can also be triggered by a previous occurrence of active imagination. So, based on our example, you now use the plane's severe shaking images in your head (which is nothing so far but active imagination) and create a new and even more frightening image. Perhaps you now imagine that some of these screaming passengers are actually crew members, which means the problem is really serious. And that shaking of the plane is causing the cabin lights in the plane to flicker. Now the plane and all the passengers are in peril!

Did any of these scary events take place? Of course not. Is your heart beating as if they actually did take place? Yes indeed.

This is what I like to refer to as the slippery-slope of the fear of flying. You partially base your existing fear of flying on a previous, but mostly made-up, scenario that was originally triggered by a very normal event. This is a downward spiral that will only increase your trepidation.

When flying, it is crucial that you do whatever you can in order to stop your active imagination. How can you eliminate active imagination from taking over your thinking processes and amplifying normal events into imaginary devastating and horrifying results? There are two methods to accomplishing that:

• Face Value Approach: This is the simpler and more logical way in dealing with active imagination. It means simply taking events at their face value. Although it is the simpler approach, it's the harder one to master, especially when onboard a plane. For example, when the seatbelt light is turned on by the pilot, you should train your brain to take this event at its face value, and stop there with the knowledge that some air turbulence will start and then end in a few short minutes. There will be no emergency, no screaming people, no certain death. If you are still concerned, take it one step further in order to comfort yourself, and investigate the situation by asking any cabin crew why the seatbelt sign was turned on. You will get the same answer, 9.99 times out of 10, and it will be something along the lines of, 'The pilot has determined that we might be crossing some turbulent weather, and this may cause the plane to shake a little bit. It's only for your safety, nothing to do with the safety of the plane itself'.

On the ground, you can more easily understand the type of person you are when it comes to active imagination. For example, when you hear a click or a bang in another room while watching TV at home, what do you do? Well, you can ignore it, or go to the other room to see what might have caused this sound, or ignite your active imagination and start thinking about how an intruder has jumped through the window into your house and that you are about to be his latest victim. So, what type of person are you? I recommend the second approach, as it is the more sensible, but doesn't require you to go into any unnecessary panic mode due to imaginary results based on your active imagination. These everyday experiences should be excellent opportunities to practice the Face Value Approach when dealing with external events.

• Super Charge Approach: If your brain starts believing the lie that your active imagination has manufactured in your brain, super charge the lie and make it a bigger one - this is the name of the game with this approach. You see, your brain will believe your imagination up to a point, but if you go beyond it, even your very own brain will tell you that it is too much to believe and will brush it off as a ridiculous thought.

This tactic should be taken only if you are not able to master the first one, which in my opinion is the better and more lasting approach. This second strategy, although practical, is more of a temporary solution than a permanent fix. But hey, whatever works to make your flight an enjoyable one. Here is how it would work: let's say that the seatbelt light turns on. Now allow your typical active imagination to work as usual, but super charge it. Start imagining ridiculous thoughts, perhaps something like the pilot has seen a UFO and he is worried that their magnetic field might impact the plane path and will cause the plane to shake. Yes, people might be screaming (original active imagination thoughts), but now they are screaming because they are worried that aliens might transport them to their ships - you can now start imagining how you will turn your head and suddenly notice that some passengers have disappeared from their seats - these UFOs are really pulling people out of the plane. A super hero must be sitting somewhere around you who will fight these aliens, and you wonder who - it must be that calm, muscular guy sitting two rows in front of you. Okay, now this is starting to sound like a comic book, but that is the whole point: things are becoming too ridiculous for your brain to believe. The most important thing here is to make the story as absurd as possible and truly live it.

PREVIOUS EXPERIENCES

So you swear that your fear is not completely baseless, and that a few years ago you had a very scary flight experience that almost ended your life and that it was a miracle that saved the plane from plunging into the ground.

Now, is that really what happened?

Are you sure?

This area of discussion can be strongly related to the previous passage on active imagination. It is worth noting that although some people might have had bad experiences in the past, the majority of us experience only typical and routine flight trips. It is not just me saying that, it is a fact based on airline safety reports.

What probably happened is that your flight ran into some air turbulence which was perhaps more severe than you were used to. But since you are a fearful flyer, your active imagination had a great opportunity to make up doomsday images and scenarios. These mental pictures can be so powerful and vivid that you may sometimes believe them over what your eyes and ears are actually seeing and hearing. So now you have a 'beefed-up' story to tell people about.

Every time you tell a friend about the incident, somehow the story becomes scarier. (Does this sound familiar?) The screaming of the passengers becomes louder, and the shaking of the plane becomes harder. The drama of your story seems to multiply by a certain factor every time you talk about it. The really interesting thing is that you will actually believe your 'new' story, and this new version of your story becomes the real one in your mind.

So when you want to get on a plane today, you will remember that previous experience but, unfortunately, you will remember the latest 'buffed-up' version, the one that the irrational part of your brain cooked up for you.

Be realistic with yourself - what really happened during that previous bad experience? Try to be honest and remember things in great detail, without coming up with conclusions or made-up thoughts. Were people actually thrown around the way you now believe they were? Are you sure you saw the engine on fire? Surely the wing didn't really crack!

Now, let's be fair and address the fact that you might very well have been on a flight that did run into extreme turbulence. In this case, yes, you did indeed have a bad experience. Can this be a reason for you to worry about your next flight? Sure. Should it? Absolutely not! And here is why. In-flight emergencies or extreme turbulence are so rare that many frequent flyers and veteran pilots have yet to experience one. So if you have actually lived through one of these incidents, the chances of it happening again are now significantly lower. In a way, your previous experience should be a comfort factor for you on your next trip. I mean, what are the chances of winning the lottery jackpot, twice?

CHAPTER TWO: COMMON CAUSES OF FEAR AND HOW TO ELIMINATE EACH ONE

IRRATIONAL EMOTIONS

Before moving any further into this book, there is a very basic but critical fact that you have to understand and truly believe, and that is the fact that your fear of flying is an irrational emotion. The key word here is irrational. This is a very important fact that I would like you to think about because it is the cornerstone to the success of any program addressing the fear of flying.

Irrational emotion means exactly that: a feeling inside you that is not based on any solid facts or real life experience. Unless you survived a plane crash or you are an aeronautic engineer who has found proof that the airline industry is hiding troublesome information about the structural reliability of its aircrafts, your fear is baseless, i.e., irrational.

The problem with irrational emotions is that they are hard to combat with opposing facts because they were never based on factual evidence in the first place. So when you read that traveling by air is one of the safest methods of getting from one point to another, somehow you will not be comforted, even though the rational part of your brain knows that this information is true. This very reassuring information about safety simply does not have an opposing fact to fight: you were never convinced that airline travel is dangerous in the first place. Whether you realize it or not, you suffer from an irrational emotion.

That is why this book touches only a little on hard statistics, and more on the practical ways of dealing with this irrational emotion. Simply put, you have heard these airline safety statistics a million times, but they have never comforted you, and they never will if that is your entire strategy to conquer your fear of flying.

In addition to reading this book, I highly encourage you to keep reminding yourself that your fear is irrational - it is baseless. If you keep reminding yourself of that, you might make a crack in the mental wall that is blocking all the rational reasons for you to fly without fear.

In addition to reminding yourself, try an exercise that might weaken that illogical mental wall. The exercise consists of questioning yourself. Ask yourself, 'Did I ever look outside the plane window and saw a fire in the engine?' 'Have I ever been on a plane that aborted the takeoff halfway down the runway, due to an emergency?' 'Did I ever experience an out of control downward free-fall while on a trip?' 'Was I ever onboard a plane where turbulence broke off any part of the wings?' 'In which case, what exactly is making me imagine and fear something that never happened and, for that matter, never happened to anyone I personally know?'

As mentioned earlier in this book, fear of flying is like a box that contains a mixture of other phobias and fears, as well as external elements that strengthen this fear. This chapter addresses the most usual components of the mixture. The six factors described are the most common reasons why people are scared to fly or ill at ease when flying. The goal of this chapter is to address each one of these factors and provide you with ways to eliminate them. By doing so, you will slowly drain your brain from the fuel that feeds your fears.

FEAR FACTORS:

- Fear of Heights (Acrophobia)

- Fear of Enclosed Places (Claustrophobia)

- Loss of Control (Symptom)

- Air Bumps – Turbulence (External element)

- Takeoff Procedure (External element)

- Unfamiliar Sounds (External element)

FEAR: HEIGHT

This is one of the more common fears that come to mind when people get asked about their fears of flying. I personally do not strongly believe that this specific fear should be part of this list, but I will address it because it is repeatedly mentioned to me by fearful flyers as a cause of anxiety. I say that because the major part of the trip duration, the plane is flying so high that a person loses their sense of height. In other words, you have no point of reference to notice how high you are (no small cars or houses can be seen).

Seeing constant blue, white, or green below you as the plane cruises at a high altitude has no relevance anymore to how high you actually are. The only time this fear can be an issue is during the takeoff and landing procedures - which I believe are triggers to a different set of fears, which I will address later in the book. This is the only time that you can look out the window and say to yourself, 'I must be a couple of hundred feet higher than this eight-story building,' for example.

Remember, we are trying to identify the actual causes of your fear of flying so they can be tackled one at a time, and this is an easy one to identify and overcome. If you worry about standing at a balcony on a taller building, or you panic when looking down the inside of a spiral staircase, then you probably suffer from acrophobia.

Prevention:

• Falling from a fourth floor balcony is not much safer than falling from 30,000 feet. So why does it feel different when you are on a plane? Ask yourself how you manage to be okay with working, visiting a friend, or staying at a hotel on an upper floor. Also, remind yourself how many times you have been in an elevator and were probably just fine with the fact that you had a good distance between you and the ground.

• Remind yourself of this fact: Planes don't just fall from the sky - the mechanics of their wings do not even allow this free fall to happen. It is a simple question of physics. Even if all the engines were to suddenly lose all power for no good reason (which, by the way, has never happened on a commercial airliner), the plane will turn into a glider and not a piece of rock falling from the sky.

• Don't think of the plane as an elevated object that you are riding, think of it as your 'new' ground, and forget about the 'old' ground (earth). These planes are so massive in size and so stable that you can easily consider them to be a ground on their own.

• Referring back to the start of this section: The only time you might notice the height is during the first few minutes or so after takeoff, and the last 20 minutes or so before landing. That's when you can actually notice the small cars and buildings which will lead to the sense of height. The way to solve this is to simply not look out the window during these minutes or, even better, close your eyes. Very simple solution.

FEAR: ENCLOSED PLACES

Fear of enclosed places, or claustrophobia, happens to some people when they feel that they are trapped in a place that is limited in size and has no easy escape route. This phobia is not limited to being inside of a plane, but to any area that makes the person who suffers from it feels entrapped. Elevators and small closets are examples of such spaces. Although not much can be done to resolve this issue onboard a plane, there are a few things that can significantly help you overcome it.

It is a very subjective phobia in my opinion. What are the dimensional limits that you would consider to be the minimal amount before you classify a space as too small? Is there a minimum height for the ceiling that, if lowered by an inch, becomes too cramped and scares you? For example, if the elevator triples in width and doubles in height would it still bother you? Would you still think of it as an elevator, or would it be a moving living room? Also, what exactly constitutes an escape route? Most elevators do have an escape hatch located on the ceiling.

Even within the claustrophobic community, opinion varies from one person to another as to whether the cabin is considered an enclosed space or not. Individual people vary, and plane sizes vary as well. Some larger jets are much bigger than our houses and the feeling of entrapment is hardly ever triggered by the closed cabin doors.

Prevention:

• Try to gain more space and room around you by getting online (or at the check-in counter) and requesting certain seats that give you more room. Some airlines charge extra for this service, but it is well worth it. Even better, reserve an exit row seat, if you can, where you will have plenty of leg room. Most airline and travel websites can now show you the seat layout of the plane.

• The ultimate solution for this issue is to book a business or first class seat. Believe me, not only will you eliminate this fear, you will develop a 'Fear of Not Flying'! Obviously (unless there are special discounts) along with your fear you might lose the money in your pocket quickly as well. So this solution has a price tag to it.

• If the above is not an option, make sure you get an aisle seat so you won't feel cramped between two people. In most cases, and pending availability, the reservation agent (or online) can make this happen at no extra charge.

• Do your homework and, if you have the flexibility, fly on larger aircraft such as Boeing 747, 777, or Airbus 340, 380. The insides of these great aircrafts are so large that it almost feels like you are in an enormous conference room or music hall. Many of the online booking services will tell you the type of aircraft used for your trip. If this fear is an issue, it is worth a bit of extra research to put yourself on one of these larger aircraft.

FEAR: LOSS OF CONTROL

In many cases, this fear applies to the same people who get nervous when they are in a car and someone else is driving. They somehow believe that they would do a better job driving themselves, and the driver is simply not doing a good job and will get into an accident at any moment.

But onboard a plane the feeling of trepidation becomes significantly greater because the situation is a bit different to being in a car. The most obvious distinction is that the sufferer not only feels the lack of control, but they don't know who is in control and whether that person is paying constant attention to what he is doing. Also, the fact that these passengers have no clue how to fly a plane makes them feel weaker and more dependent on that person (i.e., the pilot), about whom they have serious doubts to begin with.

So, with every bump or change in speed, the person who is afflicted with this particular anxiety will wonder what is going on in that small room in the front of the plane. 'I really hope they are paying attention, or are even awake,' might be a thought that comes to mind.

Prevention:

• Remember, the pilot flying the aircraft is a very experienced professional who has undergone rigorous training and has many hours of experience. This is exactly the person you want to trust and leave the controls in his or her hands. It simply does not get any more trustworthy than that.

• Luckily for you, the pilots are physically onboard with you and not flying your plane remotely from a ground control center, and they, like you, have a life and family to worry about as well. So they have the same vested interest as you do in making sure the plane takes off and lands safely.

• Another reason not to worry is that the pilot is not alone, he has a co-pilot to keep a second set of eyes and ears on the instruments. And, in some cases, there will be a third person in the cockpit acting as a relief pilot for the longer trips.

• There is one additional person (well, not really a person) that you can count on to never lose control, and that is the autopilot. This amazing computer system is considered by many professionals as the best pilot ever, watching, monitoring, and adjusting itself every second of the trip.

• Don't be fooled by the movies. The pilots are not sitting behind a closed door smoking cigarettes and laughing about their college days stories. These professionals are at work, the cockpit is their office and their flight time is their working day. They have a job to do and are busy monitoring the equipment, radar readings, listening to control tower instructions, monitoring the weather, and much more. Their communication and actions are recorded and there are consequences to any unprofessional behavior that could in any way impact flying rules and regulations.

FEAR: AIR BUMPS - TURBULENCE

The mother of all fears! This item never fails to show up on any list when it comes to fear of flying. The funny part about it is that most people who fear it and think about it all the time have little knowledge or background on what causes air bumps (turbulence). What is also funny (or sad) is that turbulence has nothing to do with in-flight risk. I personally (having done a lot of research) never heard of a plane crashing due to air bumps. So if you want to use your rational brain for a second here, there is simply zero risk due to turbulence and absolutely nothing to worry about or even discuss.

Please remember that the air is much like the sea - it is constantly moving and shifting - and in the same way that a ship moves up and down, the plane will do the same, but much less.

These bumps can be caused from wind uplift which usually happens when flying over mountains where the wind will collide with the mountains and get redirected upwards, causing it to bump your plane from below. Turbulence can also happen when the plane crosses different jet streams or flies close to storms. Whatever the reason may be, it's only the wind bumping the aircraft.

Some air bumps and shaking takes place due to flying near thunderstorms, but keep in mind that pilots are not insane and will never fly through any storm that has even the slightest chance of causing structural damage to the aircraft. The pilot will calmly request, from the ground control, permission to use a new path or different altitude to avoid these storms. In most cases, when the pilot reroutes the plane's path due to a storm, it's not because of any potential danger from the storm; he or she does it primarily for the comfort of the passengers and to avoid any disruption to passengers who are sleeping, eating, or watching a movie.

Think about it and be fair, being onboard a plane is the smoothest experience you will ever have in any motorized transportation equipment. Don't believe me? Next time you are riding (not driving) a car or a bus, close your eyes and concentrate on the bumpiness of the ride - it is not a smooth ride at all.

Prevention:

• Have you ever heard of a fatal aircraft accident due to air bumps? I personally have not. Keep that in mind when the plane shakes a little bit.

• Don't allow the 'fasten your seat belts' sign scare you when it is due to turbulence. The sign does not mean that the air bumps are dangerous to the aircraft. It simply means that the captain is concerned about passengers who may not be safely fastened in their seats falling down or hurting themselves.

• Many captains (and folks that do not fear flying) do not even notice light or moderate bumps, the very same bumps that make you panic. It is similar to how you would not notice minor ups and downs when riding a car. Your fear and mental state makes a much bigger deal out of it.

• Related to the above item, when air bumps begin, try to look around and see if you can find a passenger who appears not to have even noticed the bump and who is comfortably napping or quietly reading a book. By the way, you will find many of these passengers around you. This should indicate to you that everything is alright. It will also relax you a little bit.

• Most air bumps are light to moderate. Extreme turbulence is so rare that many pilots with several years of flying under their belts have never even experienced it.

• Once you get over this specific fear, you will find that air bumps are the best way to gently rock you into a nice and comfortable nap.

FEAR: TAKEOFF PROCEDURE

The takeoff procedure is a hard one to swallow for many people who fear flying. The complete silence followed by the sudden roar of the engines, and then the rushing speed.

Although every step of this procedure is normal and happens thousands of times every day, it is not a natural feeling for us humans, and some of us take it a step further to where any anxiety becomes a full-blown fear.

Remember that this is the way airplanes have taken off since the dawn of aviation and it is very normal - this machine was designed specifically to takeoff this way.

The sounds of these engines should never scare you; they are simply mighty powerful but have an annoyingly loud noise. The pilot and co-pilot have a check list to go over before flying, ensuring that all systems are working properly. They even have a special procedure in case of the (extremely rare) need to abort the takeoff.

A few seconds after takeoff, some people report the feeling of falling downwards. If you watch the informational screen, on the back of the seat in front of you or above the aisles, which shows the altitude, you will notice that the plane is constantly climbing to its set altitude - nothing is falling down. So why do you feel like you're falling? It is usually due to what is known as the decrease rate of climbing. When the pilot decreases the rate of climbing (still climbing, but not as aggressively), a natural feeling of falling down takes place. Think of the elevator; let's say you are on the 1st floor and you press the 8th floor button - shortly before you arrive at the 8th floor, the elevator slows down (although it is still actually moving upwards), which gives you a brief sensation of falling downwards. This is exactly the same action taking place when you get this feeling during takeoff.

Prevention:

• The Internet has many posted videos from inside the cockpit during takeoff. I strongly recommend watching some of them because it will show you that while you are sitting in the back of plane, panicking, the pilots are completely calm and confident.

• Close your eyes and take deep breaths.

• Concentrate on a totally different subject, preferably a pleasant one. Something like your destination, who and what you will see. You only need to kill a few seconds.

• If you cannot get your mind off the takeoff, start visualizing the dozens of planes that you saw taking off while waiting in the terminal before boarding. You saw so many of them, and it looked so routine, that it became a boring repetitive scene. Well, you are now in one of those planes doing that same boring routine called takeoff, and someone else inside the terminal is watching your plane takeoff and thinking of how dull it is.

FEAR: UNFAMILIAR SOUNDS

This is the item that I refer to as the 'Art School'- because it makes every person who fears flying an audio artist with a great skill set of imagination and creativity. It sounds a bit funny, but it is so true. Here is what I mean; if you are driving and hear a strange sound when the car is shifting gears, you will either just ignore it as a normal new sound, or assume the gear needs some kind of maintenance sometime soon - and your thoughts probably end there.

But onboard a plane, if you hear any sound, your new artistic imagination skills will start thinking that perhaps a bird hit the plane, or a piece of the plane's body broke and fell off, or the engine is just about to stop working, or the wing might break off.... and the funny (or sad) thing is that you build on that 'made up' assumption, and start considering the consequences of this fault in the plane. (Remember our discussion about active imagination?) You actually might even prepare yourself for an emergency, because that sound, which your brain decided was dangerous, has caused an 'imaginary' body/engine problem, leading to an emergency. Wow, now that's the kind of artistic skill that is very much in demand only in Hollywood.

Prevention:

• The plane has hundreds of moving parts. It is very normal for these moving parts to make sounds. Honestly, I would be worried if no sounds were produced during takeoff.

• Unless you are an aircraft mechanic or have built airplanes before, you simply do not know what is a 'normal' versus an 'abnormal' sound. So give your nervous system a break and don't pretend that you can be the judge of these sounds. Considering the overwhelming percentage of successful takeoffs versus problematic ones, the chances are well over 99.99% that the sounds you are hearing are perfectly normal.

• Again, go to online video postings of takeoffs and watch them at a high volume to hear the sounds. These videos should help you prepare yourself for takeoff by expecting these sounds to happen.

CHAPTER THREE: PREPARING YOURSELF TO FLY AGAIN

Now that we have addressed the most common fears of flying and provided practical suggestions to eliminate each one of them, we can move on to the next step, which is preparing yourself for a flight.

The work to conquer this fear starts at the time you decide to fly, and ends in the phase that discusses what you should do onboard the plane.

Try not to miss any of these steps, at least for the first trip or two. I would even recommend doing these steps for every planned trip until the fear is completely gone. Simply treat it as you would treat a dietary program - step by step without skipping any.

The 'Preparing yourself for a fear-free flight' program is divided into four phases, divided as follows:

Phase I – Pre-Booking: When You Decide to Take a Flight, Up Until Booking.

Phase II – Post-Booking: After You Book the Flight, Before Travel Day.

Phase III – Travel Day: Prior to Boarding the Plane.

Phase IV – Onboard the Plane.

PHASE ONE: WHEN YOU DECIDE TO TAKE A FLIGHT, UP UNTIL BOOKING

Read about airline safety record.

Get on the internet and search for words such as 'flight safety record'. You will find several web sites that have statistics on flight safety, organized by region, airline, and plane types.

Look up incidents in the last 10 years, and you will see for yourself how rare it is for an accident to take place. They are so infrequent; most of these statistics are measured by every million takeoffs. Simply put, the number will be negligible if measured by, let's say, every 10,000 takeoffs. That should speak volumes for the safety of airlines.

But don't stop there; these numbers (although low) are very deceiving. Figures usually will include minor incidents (planes landing relatively close to other aircrafts, wings accidentally touching a foreign object while taxiing, etc.). In other words, these already very low numbers include incidents that do not constitute any true threat to the aircraft, and many of them happened while the plane was still on the ground.

More importantly, a large percentage of these rare incidents involve airlines with less than perfect reputations with regard to their maintenance standards. Without mentioning any airline by name (you will find out yourself), the chances are that you will not fly on these airlines in the first place. Such aircraft do not belong to US based airliners or to any western European country. So please pay attention to the airlines when looking up historic statistics.

After reading these statistics, you will realize how unusual it is for a reputable airline to be involved in a fatal accident. Very few and far between! You have to go back so many years, and so many millions of takeoffs before you can use all your fingers to count them.

Pay attention to the daily news

Start paying attention to the news; the chances are you will be an expert in local and global economic and political matters before you hear about a commercial airline incident.

We have discussed earlier how the media is starved of dramatic stories to report on. So how come you are now so bored from watching the news and never hearing a single word about an airline accident? The simple answer is that airlines are so safe, even reporters hungry for flashy news cannot find something to report on.

One last note on this topic: While wasting your time watching the news and waiting to hear about any airline incident, have you noticed how many fatal car accidents were announced? The point here being, you are safer onboard a plane than on the highway. So unless you are willing to develop a fear of driving, your fear of flying does not really make any sense. Another important tip - be careful driving your car to the airport as that will be the most dangerous part of your trip, no joke.

Read about the number of daily takeoffs and landing

According to the internet site for the National Air Traffic Controllers Association, there are over 87,000 flights in the skies of the United States alone on any given day, and roughly 5,000 of these flights are over the same skies at any given moment. If you add up the numbers, this means that there are on average 64 million takeoffs and landings every single year. These are very large numbers.

So the chances are that there will be over a million flights that will takeoff and land safely between this day and your planned trip date. Why do you feel yours will be any different?

There have been some studies that show the odds of being killed on a single trip on a top 25 airline flight are 1 in 9 million. In my mind, this number tells me that there are roughly 8,999,999 other things in life I need to worry about before worrying about dying on an airplane.

I totally understand that these numbers are statistics only, and the fear of flying is more of an irrational emotion than a realistic fear. But please stop for a second and use the rational part of your brain when looking at these numbers - they are very powerful.

Pick a route that has the least stops, on larger aircraft, and with a reputable airline.

If you go back only 15 years, when airlines actually had offices in buildings, you had no idea what aircraft equipment type you were going to board. For those who feared flying, they simply hoped it would not be a little plane.

With the age of the internet and online reservations, most booking sites will tell you the exact route and the aircraft equipment that will be used.

So why don't you use this information to your advantage? In many cases, airlines will fly different routes on different equipment for the same destination. I recommend taking the most direct route if available (non-stop), and choosing one of the larger airlines as many people with a fear of flying feel more comfortable with the larger interior space.

Shop for items that will entertain you the most on the plane

Here is an excuse to spend some money at the mall. Think of
your favorite time-killing product - a fashion magazine; a
portable video game; the latest electronic gadget, or a good
relaxing book. (Just make sure you obey the flight crew
instructions when using any electronic devices.)

For a person who fears flying, it will be very hard to do
anything while on the plane- especially during takeoff or
turbulence - even if it was their favorite thing in the world to
do when not onboard. So this step might help you pass some
time during your flight, but only when it's a smooth flight at a
cruising altitude.

I want to be realistic with you; don't force yourself into
trying to enjoy some sort of hobby while the plane is hitting
any air bumps. In my opinion, it will just make you more
nervous. Again, this step is useful during smooth flying as a
way to pass the time.

Purchase a sound canceling headphone for your MP3/iPod player

Once you have clearance from the cabin crew to use
electronic devices, I strongly recommend using a high quality
sound canceling headphone to use with your favorite MP3
player.

In my opinion, this is a very important step to take. A good sound canceling headphone will accomplish three things:

1- You will not hear the roaring of the engine anymore, which in turn will help you mentally distance yourself from the fact that you are onboard a plane. More importantly, many people who fear flying imagine and report a change in the sound of the engine while in the air. Although this might be true due to a change of speed or altitude, in most cases it is actually their imagination at work, and the brain trying to prove to the owner of that brain that he or she is right, and that something is actually wrong with the aircraft. Using these sound cancelling headphones will prevent you from hearing (or imagining) these noise variations.

2-You will not hear the clicks and clacks of the bathroom doors and the kitchen cabinets. These sounds are nothing to worry about, but for someone who fears flying they are incentives to panic.

3-The music you listen to should relax you and put your mind at ease - putting you in a totally different state of mind or reminding you of pleasurable events in your life. Whatever it does, it is also distancing you from the fact that you are onboard a plane.

Although sound canceling headphones are great, please remember that you might not hear the beep that goes along with the captain's request to fasten your seat belts or any other instructions. So always keep your seat belt on (something you should do, regardless, during the entire trip). Just stay vigilant, but not nervous for any instructions by the captain or the cabin crew.

Reserve comfortable seats through the airline web site

Here is another important step, yet an easy one. Again, due to the internet age and online booking, most airlines will allow you (sometimes for a fee) to choose the seat you want. Use this feature to your advantage, and as a person who is trying to conquer their fear of flying, it is worth every dollar spent on this service.

Unless you are one of the few lucky ones who can afford to fly business or first class, the seat you will be allocated will not offer you much legroom. For the folks who fear flying, being in an enclosed space makes matter worse for them. So try to choose a front row (or exit row) seat. Some airlines reserve these seats for people with special needs or parents with infants, and the airline might have special instructions for the holders of the exit row seats, but it is worth a try.

If you are not able to get these front row seats with the extra leg room, I recommend getting an aisle seat as that will give you the feeling of extra space (the aisle).

From my experience and the experience of people I have asked, the seats in the middle of the plane (front to back), above the wings, experience the least amount of bumpiness during rough weather. This could be related to the fact that they are closest to the center of gravity of the aircraft body.

So the combination of front row seats (or exit seats if possible), aisle seats, and being in the middle of the aircraft are your best bet for the most comfortable ride.

Wake up as early as possible

I don't have any scientific reason for this step, except I like to do it because by the time I board the plane I will be very tired and sleepy due to waking up so early, thereby increasing my chances of falling asleep during the flight.

You might hear some people suggest that having a good night's sleep and getting to the airport fully awake and alert is a good way to conquer your fear. I will not argue with people who hold this belief, and it is something you may want to try. It is just in my opinion and experience, sleeping onboard a plane becomes more possible when I am tired, and will make the flight seem shorter.

Arrive at the airport and check in early

Some people recommend that I get to the airport as late as possible so I don't think about the flight. I disagree, because you will think about your flight that day, regardless of your location. So go to the airport early as this will give you enough time to do the next two steps.

Find a good viewing area and watch planes takeoff and land

Remember the statistics discussed earlier? Well, now you have a chance to visualize a piece of it. In a busy or reasonably busy airport you will be able to see a plane taking-off every few minutes.

Look at each plane as it takes-off and see how routine the process is. Chase the plane visually until it disappears in the air or becomes a small dot in the sky, at which point you can turn your attention to the next takeoff.

Imagine yourself in each of these planes, how nervous you would be when you are inside it - the speed, the sounds of the flaps, and the roaring engine. Now, think about what you are actually looking at - a smooth and ordinary takeoff which is almost boring to watch.

As you observe each plane, continue to switch between these two different roles, one as an observer of a commonplace and mundane takeoff, and the other as a passenger inside that plane.

Now, promise yourself that you will remember this typical scene during your flight's takeoff as if you were watching it from the waiting area.

Talk to the pilot before boarding

If you can, try to locate your pilot (they usually arrive with their crew and head towards your boarding gate entrance). Don't be shy, pilots are very nice and understanding. Tell him or her that you will be onboard their flight and you have a fear of flying. Tell them exactly what bothers you (takeoff, air bumps...etc.).

From my personal experience in doing so, most pilots would spend several minutes explaining to me the nature of these sounds and the reasons behind the bumps. It is so comforting to hear it from the pilot. Notice how comfortable they are when talking about these matters; it is no different to them than a child asking you about the danger of street bumps when driving a car.

PHASE FOUR: ONBOARD THE PLANE

Keep looking at the cabin crew

One thing I recommend while boarding the plane and walking through the aisle to find your seat is to keep looking at the cabin crew. Notice how they are smiling and pleasant (well, we can only hope), but more importantly, notice how comfortable they are and busy doing their work.

The purpose of this exercise is to mentally help you realize that everything is fine and will continue to be so; otherwise these trained experts would have left the plane while they still could. If these people working onboard had anything to worry about, they would not be comfortable, smiling, and going along doing their normal work.

Ask yourself why you can't be like them? If these folks are okay, is it possible that your fear is irrational? Or you can take a different approach and think of the number of trips the crew has to take in the next few days, while you are lucky enough to only have this trip to worry about.

Either way, the only negative side effect of doing this exercise is the risk of being considered rude for staring at people. Oh well, your cause is bigger - they will just have to learn to live with you for the duration of the trip.

Sit comfortably and relax

Being uncomfortable in the way you sit will just add more stress, so get yourself in a comfortable position. Whether you like to grab and hold the pillow, cross your hands, or cross your legs at the ankle - do whatever you need to do in order to feel cozy.

Do not think about the takeoff

Whatever you do while in your seat, do not think about the takeoff. Thinking about it is a sure way to increase your heart rate, which will in turn increase your anxiety and fear.

Get yourself busy while waiting for the takeoff. I have read several articles regarding the fear of flying subject and many suggest thinking of pleasant thoughts. Although it is a great idea, my practical experience has proved to me that it is very hard to think of anything pleasant when you are anxious or worried. So I recommend thinking about serious matters, such as asking yourself whether you locked the door when you left the house. Do you have your passport or IDs with you? Did you confirm your car rental or hotel reservations? What will your workday be like the next morning? Did you say anything inappropriate to any co-workers before leaving? Or to a family member you will be seeing at your destination? Etc.,etc.

In my opinion, these are more powerful and necessary thoughts than the miscellaneous happy thoughts, so they have a much better chance of overpowering your worries about the plane and the takeoff that is about to start.

Snap out of any negative thoughts immediately

The brain of the person who fears flying works in a very strange way - the thoughts are progressive and each negative and irrational thought is built on a previous negative and irrational thought. In other words, your thoughts advance and build on top of each other at a very fast pace. (Remember active imagination?)

To clarify it further, your first irrational thought might be imagining that during the takeoff you will hear a strange engine sound, and the next thought might be how you will look out the window while the plane starts to climb and you will see a fire in one of the engines, and the next thought could be imagining how the plane will tilt to one side and instead of seeing the horizon from your window, you will see only the ground while objects are flying in the cabin and people are screaming. These are irrational thoughts that are built on false assumptions and powered by your active imagination, leading to imagining a false sequence of events.

So as a person who fears flying, one negative thought is bad news for you because it will not end at that thought but will lead to another. Therefore, you have to prevent these negative thoughts immediately as they arise. Consider this advice as a must-follow rule, a very critical one.

I recommend three different ways to prevent this dangerous downward spiral of thoughts:

1- The simplest way is to remind yourself to immediately stop thinking in a pessimistic way, and also to remind yourself that you have read and realize that what you're doing is based on completely false assumptions and that you have to stop now. You must change what's going on in your mind and immediately think of something else, anything unrelated to flying such as, 'Did I bring my laptop or cell phone with me?' Or maybe, 'Did I pack enough underwear for the trip?' Anything will work.

2-Don't hurt yourself, but some people put a rubber band around their wrist and anytime these damaging thoughts come to mind, they snap it against their wrist while reminding themselves to think of something else. It's a way to literally snap out of such thoughts.

3-I like to refer to this final method as the cartoon approach. This is done by adding extra, and very unrealistic, details to your existing active imagination to the point where your brain will brush aside these thoughts as ridiculous. For example, when you start imagining that the engine is making a strange and unfamiliar sound, construct your next thought to be something like imagining a 'spare' engine which will be automatically extracted from below the engine with a sign that says 'super engine', and that second engine will be so strong that it will make the plane takeoff like a rocket, so fast that in two seconds you will be over the clouds. Now repeat that thought with three new engines, or maybe a laser-powered beam coming from the wings to help the plane fly - whatever your funny imagination can come up with. Not only will such thoughts dilute the believability of your active imagination, they will also pass the time and amuse you.

Think of all the research you have already done

If the previous step did not work and you had to think about the takeoff, remind yourself of all the research you have made in the days leading up to your trip. Also, remember the routine and boring takeoffs you saw while waiting in the terminal.

Remember, there are thousands of safe takeoffs that took place since you boarded your plane and yours will be just another one of those.

Close your eyes

Whether you managed to distract yourself from any flight-related thoughts, or were simply thinking of how safe takeoff is - keep your eyes closed.

By closing your eyes you will prevent yourself from looking out the window which, to many people who fear flying, is a cause for them to feel more nervous.

If you could not close your eyes, I strongly recommend repeating an earlier exercise, and that is looking at the closest cabin crew. Their facial expressions will speak volumes on how unconcerned they are and that there is nothing about the flight that is worrying them.

Expect some bumps

A few air bumps and some shaking of the plane are natural occurrences. Do expect them to take place and, when it happens, tell yourself, "Yup, as expected, here are the few bumps that normally happen.", and when they stop, tell yourself, "Okay, first batch of bumps has gone, let's see when the next batch of bumps will start again."

Keep in mind that the wind is out there and is moving, and that will shake the plane a little bit. It should not surprise you - and for sure should not worry you. Just like the sea wave will shake the ship a little bit, these air waves will do the same - it is all very natural.

A comfortable flyer might not even notice these bumps. I have flown with people that wondered what I was talking about when I reminded them of the shaking that took place during the takeoff. Do you remember every minor bump on the road when you drive? It's no different to them, and should not be any different to you.

Expect unfamiliar sounds

Similar to the point above, you should also expect some unfamiliar sounds during takeoff. Actually, these sounds should be comforting, ensuring you that normal takeoff procedures are taking place.

For example, the gear has to go up (pulling the plane wheels up); this mechanical function will make a sound during the wheel retraction and possibly a thump sound as the wheel door latches.

Another natural sound is the movement of the flaps. The flaps are the moving parts at the end of the wings. They help the plane takeoff and have to be at a different position once the plane is at a certain altitude. Again, this is a mechanical function, and the retraction of the flaps will make a sound which is no cause for alarm.

Expect fluctuation in the speed

This one almost never fails to scare those who have a fear of flying - the change in the sound of the engine (getting quieter). A person who fears flying and is not educated enough about planes will immediately think that the engine is failing - this is not the case at all.

In some cases, pilots do indeed reduce the engine thrust shortly after takeoff, but this is done intentionally. Their decision to do so can be attributed to many reasons, such as flying over some populated cities that enforce noise regulations, which require the pilot to reduce the thrust to quieten the sound of the engine so the residents below can take a break from these loud noises. Of course the pilot might be reducing the thrust because he or she does not need the same level of engine power that was required during the first few seconds of the takeoff procedure.

Whatever the reason, relax - nothing is failing.

Expect to feel that the plane is losing altitude during takeoff

Similar to the point above, it's another common item that folks who fear flying report in many of their trips - and that is the feeling of the loss of altitude during takeoff.

I cannot say that their feeling is wrong, because it is a true feeling indeed. But is the plane actually losing altitude? No. So why do they get this feeling?

The explanation of this phenomenon is described earlier in this book. But as a reminder, it is the same feeling you get when the elevator that is taking you up in a building approaches its destination floor. As it approaches, the elevator slows down (decreases its rate of climb). This decrease rate of climb makes you feel as if you are falling downwards, but in reality, you are still moving upwards.

Remember, your pilot is not taking you to the moon, and sooner or later the plane will approach its designated altitude and the pilot will have to decrease the rate of his climb to level the plane off. It is also possible that the ground control requests that the pilot slows down the climb rate due to air traffic above the plane, a routine procedure to ensure safety distances are maintained between planes.

This point and the one prior to it are sometimes related and can happen at the same time, which will create a bigger reason for the person who fears flying to be irrationally concerned. If the pilot decided to reduce the engine thrust (previous point), the plane naturally might climb at a lower rate.

CHAPTER FOUR: LET YOUR BRAIN DO THE WORK

This chapter will discuss certain features of the human brain that you can utilize to end your fear of flying. As promised at the beginning of this book, we will not dive into any medical terms but rather we will talk about brain features that you use unconsciously on a regular basis without ever considering their power to help you overcome your anxieties.

BRAINS DO NOT LIKE TO BE CONFUSED

Your brain simply does not like being confused; it will always try to sort things out in a logical manner. It likes to classify things and events as safe, dangerous, hot, cold...etc. If a certain item or event is giving your brain conflicting signals, your brain becomes confused and it will try very hard to figure out the actual nature of the event in a logical way. You can capitalize on this feature of your brain by putting it in a confusing situation and letting it do the work for you.

For example, let's say that you are outside a lion's cage at the zoo and, while admiring this wild animal, you notice a person inside the cage with his back to the lion, doing some maintenance work to the cage. Your first reaction might be panic or suspense; you might even point your finger at that person and tell the person next to you, "Oh, is it okay for this guy to be in there with the lion?" or, "I don't think this guy noticed that the lion in the cage is roaming free". Your brain is now in the 'Imminent Danger' mode. But then you turn around and see everyone else is smiling and taking pictures and even the zoo keeper is looking and does not seem to be worried. What you are seeing now reflects a 'No Danger' mode to your brain. So which one is it? Your brain has to find an answer to this confusing situation!

In this case for example you will either have to inquire about the situation, use some logic, or remember some facts you already know to neutralize the circumstances so your brain can take one side or another - danger or safety! So you might ask the zoo keeper about the situation and she will tell you that there is actually a glass barrier between the maintenance guy and the lion, or your own logic or previous knowledge will tell you that the lion must have been fed recently and cares less about the maintenance guy (lunch) being around. Either way, you satisfied your brain's need to classify the position you are in.

Now, does this example relate to your fear of flying? Yes, it does! You see, as a fearful flyer, your irrational emotions have programmed your brain into believing that flying is putting you in a dangerous situation. So you will probably continue to be fearful about flying as long as your brain sees no conflicting or confusing signals that are the opposite of that, i.e. a safe situation.

Now, let's confuse your brain a little bit and introduce it to some true physical evidence (not merely some safety statistics prepared by someone else) that the situation is actually very safe, similar to the safe and comforting scene when you looked at the people around you at the zoo, in the lion example above.

Next time you are at the airport waiting to board your flight, look around you. Do you see scared people, or people either talking on their cell phones, completing crosswords, reading a book, or listening to music on their MP3 players?

If you see scared people, then maybe you are right to be scared about flying and perhaps you should consider driving a car instead next time you want to be somewhere. But I assure you that you will not see scared people, you will see people busy with their personal activities as if they were about to board a bus.

Everything you will see around you indicates to your brain that the situation you are in should be classified as 'safe'. Now your brain is confused between a 'dangerous' or a 'safe' situation, so who will prevail? Well, usually I would say that the physical evidence around you will win out, but since the fear of flying is pretty powerful, your brain might resist the evidence your own eyes are witnessing. Reading this book and following its instructions will provide your brain with enough support to increase its chances of siding with the physical evidence you will see around you, the 'safe' environment.

The same experience can happen onboard the plane; look around you after you are seated. Again, I assure you that you will see some people comfortably resting, even falling asleep. Goodness, you will find people completely asleep while the plane is taking off! Listen to your brain, it's trying to tell you that based on everything it sees, things are okay and safe - and they really are.

It is easier said than done, but if you keep looking around and paying attention to people's faces and actions and think about how relaxed they are, your brain will start adjusting itself to the 'everything is okay' mode. Your brain's only enemy at this point of time is you, because you are going against your brain's natural way of thinking.

Day dreaming is sometimes one of our best tools to mentally escape our current situation or location and be somewhere else through our vivid imagination. Some of us are better at day dreaming than others, but one thing is common - the outside elements while we are day dreaming play a major role in how realistic the feeling of being somewhere else becomes.

For example, if you wanted to day dream about your favorite ski resort cabin, enjoying the serene cold winter, it would be hard to do so while waiting at a bus stop in the middle of a very hot day, a loud construction site behind you, and exhaust smoke from cars filling your lungs. Day dreaming about your favorite ski resort under these circumstances is impossible, or at best, would not feel real at all.

But let's take the example above and just change the elements around you when you day dream. Your favorite vacation spot is still that wonderful ski resort cabin, and that is still exactly what you want to day dream about. Except in this case, you are waiting at a bus stop around 8pm on a cold December night on a less-travelled road. You close your eyes, and suddenly your imagination is so much more realistic. That cold breeze feels just like the one at the ski resort and the serenity is identical.

In both examples above, you had identical day dreams, just different external elements. But the difference between the results of the first and second scenario was significant. This was successfully accomplished due to the support of the elements you were in (calmness and cold weather in this example). With the support of the external elements, you mentally transported yourself from your current location to the ski resort, from A to B.

To relate the above to fear of flying - when you get on an airplane, you will need to mentally transport yourself, through day dreaming, to a place or situation that you consider safe, in such a convincing way that you feel as if you are not onboard a plane anymore. Just like the above ski resort cabin example, your best chance of success at this mental transportation is to find another situation that shares external elements with flying.

So what shares elements with being on a plane and is safe? Cars!

Your goal on the plane is to transport yourself from your current situation (being on a plane) to another, pleasant situation (being in a car on a beautiful sea-side road), by utilizing some of the events (external elements) during the flight that share characteristics with the external elements of the pleasant situation. In other words, use these 'scary' events to your very advantage.

For example, a bumpy flight might be very similar to the bumps you would feel on the road (although roads are much bumpier than a plane ride). So you close your eyes and imagine yourself in a car driving on a very beautiful coastline road on a sunny day. And every time the plane hits an air bump, you (in your day dream) look at the road ahead of you to check on the road's surface. Yes, live the experience - live the day dream. How about the incline during takeoff, are you starting to take the scenic route into the mountain?

The common in-flight events listed below are compared to similar ones that take place during a normal car ride. The goal of this illustration is to prove to you that you are completely fine dealing with so many events as long as they don't happen during a flight, even if they were identical. Why so bias? Ever asked yourself that question? If not, please do. I hope your answer will revolve around the fact that the events are not the root cause of your fear- it is your irrational emotions that link these, otherwise very normal events by your very own account, to potentially dangerous outcomes.

EVENT: Bumpy rides

On the road: There is no silk-road. Notice how most streets make your car vibrate, ups and downs, or even sudden jolts. This bumpy feeling is very natural and expected when a car is moving (or any object for that matter). Unless you are paying attention to it, you will never notice it.

On the plane: Sometime during the flight the plane shakes a little due to air turbulence. In most cases, they are minor bumps here and there. So why is this suddenly unacceptable to you now?

EVENT: Speed variance

On the road: Using highway ramps and exits to enter or leave a highway is all about changing your speeds. Even the sound of your car's engine changes when doing so.

On the plane: Specifically during takeoff and landing procedures, you will feel a change in the speed of the plane - sometimes (and naturally so) accompanied with a corresponding engine sound change.

EVENT: Seat belt light on

On the road: Wait a minute! You have to fasten your seatbelt the entire time you are driving. That seatbelt light is always On when you drive a car.

On the plane: During takeoff, landing, and bumpy phases of the trip, the pilot requests that the passengers fasten their seatbelt to comply with flight regulations and reduce the risk of accidental injury from falling or hitting nearby objects. How come this only 'sometimes On' seatbelt light that is meant to prevent a very rare and hardly-ever serious injuries is of a major concern to you?

EVENT: Unfamiliar or unknown sounds

On the road: When you buy (or borrow) a car, you may hear unfamiliar engine sounds. Unless you have a reason to believe otherwise, you will assume that they are normal sounds for this vehicle.

On the Plane: During takeoff or landing, you may hear some unfamiliar sounds, usually related to retraction of the plane wheels or flaps. As a non-expert, why assume these sounds are not normal?

CONCLUSION

By now you should know that your fear of flying has little to do with the safety of the commercial airline industry and that there is no such thing as a single and independent phobia called "Fear of Flying". Your fear of flying has everything to do with other phobias such as heights and enclosed places, or external elements such as negative media or the typical sounds an airplane produces during its normal course of flight.

Also, you now have the how-to knowledge to counterattack your fears of flying with knowledge, practical tips, and strategies on how to utilize some of your existing brain power and thinking patterns.

Hopefully within a very short period of time you will be a fearless flyer, visiting family and friends, conducting business, and seeing new places. I strongly recommend that you fly, and fly as often as you can financially afford to. The great U.S. poet, Ralph Waldo Emerson, stated, "Do the things we fear, and the death of fear is certain."

You will be glad you took the effort to rid yourself of this fear as there is just so much to do and see in your life time.

See you onboard!

48809384R00041